RIDE O~

Claire

M~~~. ~~.

Gillie,

Warm winter stars
and cool Summer
moon to follow
you on your journey.

Claire
X

RIDE ON
after the song 'Ride On' by Christy Moore

ISBN: 0-9526432-6-X

Illustrations by Lara Varga
Design by Glenn Carmichael
Photograph of Author by Paul Deaton

Published by
PotA Press

Acknowledgements
'The Unanswerable Question II' published by *Iota Magazine* (2005), 'The Hippocrene' published by *Agenda Magazine* (2005), 'Bubbles' shortlisted for the Wells Poetry Prize (2004), 'When I Heard the News' presented as part of *Dock Stories*, a project by Anna Oliver and part of the Dialogue artists project

Thanks
To Carcanet Press for permission to use a quotation from Oscar Wilde's 'The Ballad of Reading Gaol'; to Great Ormond Street Hospital for Children, for excerpts from *Peter Pan* © 1937, London; to Random House Group for excerpts from 'We are many' by Pablo Neruda, published by Jonathan Cape.

Love and Thanks
To Paul Curtis, Fiona Hamilton, Will Heath, Nicola Padden and Richard Williams

THE HIPPOCRENE - THE HORSE WELL
for Nick

At last you are Pegasus
with wings strong enough to carry you
to the heavens.
I hear their rhythm
in my dreams like sonnets.

You are the mare
who destroys mercifully.
You have killed yourself
and saved me.

Before you left
your stomping hooves
dug out the hippocrene
in the shape of a crescent moon.

Now I stoop on my knees to drink.
The well is deep.
My cupped hands run over
with inspiration.

The hands that wished
they'd held your hand
as you snorted and stamped the air
as you turned from man
into a flying horse.

For Jake, with love

Preface

RIDE ON by Claire Williamson is not exactly the kind of poetry book you might be used to reading. Most people I've asked tell me when they pick up a book of poems they don't, as a rule, begin at the beginning and read all the way through to the end in the way that they would a story or a novel, but rather dip in and out, perhaps the title of a particular poem catches the eye, or it's a line baited with an image too tempting to be resisted. But RIDE ON is not that kind of book of poems. It is, in part, the story of Claire Williamson's life, and it really should be read as a story, from beginning to end.

The first time I read RIDE ON I did so in one - *ignore the ringing phone and the knocking on the door and the coffee in the cup and the much loved Christy Moore album, from which this book takes it's name, playing in the background, totally riveted from first to final page -* ninety-minute sitting. It is easy to read. It's a page-turner. It is such an unforgettable and thrilling ride, though sometimes it's shocking and painfully sad. It's a story told in poems of three bright, imaginative children growing up in a household of secrets. It's a story of repression, resentment and guilt, where uncommon violence was commonplace, yet would often come when least expected. It's a story of a circle of revelations and consequences.

In some ways it's like a detective story and may be compared to those rare novels in verse such as *The Monkey's Mask* (Serpent's Tail) by Dorothy Porter, and *Lara* (Angela Royal Publishing) by Bernadine Evaristo. Poets such as Jackie Kay in the *Adoption Papers* (Bloodaxe); Pascale Petit in *The Zoo Father* (Seren); Pamela Gillilan in *That Winter* (Bloodaxe) and Mahendra Solanki in *What You Leave Behind* (Blackwater Books) have also explored aspects and areas of their own lives and experience in a very honest, direct and auto-biographical way, as does, in prose, Andrea Ashworth in *Once in a House on Fire* (Owl Books).

Poetry can take many forms but must always be more than the unloading of one's head or one's heart upon a page. Poetry is more than catharsis. It is ultimately, for Claire Williamson, about communication: communication with the self, the unconscious, and with other people. RIDE ON speaks and sings and dances with the reader through images and metaphors and word play and story. And though the story told contains some terribly heart-rending events and revelations it also holds humour and laughter and moments of loving kindness and solidarity to set against stupidity, selfishness, violence and despair.

Claire Williamson writes both poetry and prose, she is much in demand as a performer, as a host at poetry events and as a workshop leader. She often works in schools because she believes in introducing and sharing the process of poetry with children and young people. She also works with adults in a variety of educational contexts including using autobiographical writing to help people make sense of their past and current lives.

The title of this book is well chosen indeed, on so many levels, for it is most certainly an incredible gallop for life, born out of death.

Saddle up, compañeros and hold on tight...

Colin Brown
Director, Poetry Can

RIDE ON

Claire Williamson

CONTENTS

The Hippocrene – The Horse Well

MOTHERMOTHER

Sandy Street

17 - Seven Years
18 - The Sun Has Got His Hat On
19 - Bambi
20 - The Name Guessing Game
21 - Daddy
22 - The Unanswerable Question
23 - The Games We Play
24 - After Muchos Somos
25 - Bubbles
27 - Rosettes I
29 - Singing Our Hearts Out
30 - Mike
31 - Taking The Heat Off
32 - Pointing
33 - Bone Idle

'What you don't know…'

37 - Leaving
38 - The Night They Came
39 - Dogged
40 - The Silver Tassie
41 - The Legacy
42 - The Black Eye
43 - Alice in Wonderland
45 - Artificial Intelligence
46 - Letting the Cat Out of the Bag

Blackbird Hall

51 - Moving
52 - London Zoo
54 - A Fistful of Flowers
55 - Wiping the Slate Clean
56 - Domesticity
57 - All About My Mother
58 - Wouldn't you just die without Mahler?

59 - The Other Half
61 - Leaving Home

Searching
65 - Wicked Step-Mother
66 - Womankind
67 - Are you Ready?
69 - Diary on Amalfi Beach
70 - Fingers Crossed
71 - The Geese are Heading Home
74 - The Welcome Party
76 - Enough
77 - Seafield Crematorium
78 - Long Distance Love
79 - Worcester
81 - Delegation
82 - The Mother-Mother Tree

BROTHER

Nick
88 - When I Heard the News
90 - Stari Most (Old Bridge)
92 - An Empty Catkin
93 - Ride On I
95 - Haiku
96 - West Hope
101 - Knocking
102 - Haiku
103 - Venice
106 - The Unanswerable Question II
108 - You Can't Judge a Book by its Cover
109 - When They Heard the News

The Journey
113 - Am I Ready?
114 - Rosettes II
116 - Two Not One
117 - Ride On II

MOTHERMOTHER

Sandy Street

Seven Years

We are going to Tunisia tomorrow
and I am crying into my duvet
afraid of aeroplanes, or scorpions, or something.

Mummy comes in
kneels at my side
hand smoothing my forehead
pushing blonde hair back against the pillow
puffing into a crown of soothing words
about a vast heated swimming pool
gardens full of orange and lemon trees
which smell like sweeties
and grow on forever
until they reach the beach
where horses and camels
wait in tasselled head-dresses
to take us on magical rides
until I fall asleep
no longer frightened
of aeroplanes, or scorpions, or anything.

THE SUN HAS GOT HIS HAT ON

The sun is in the pool.
Hedgehogs, wolf spiders and leaves
are skimmed from the surface.
The marbled plastic interior washed
with a fine-haired brush like a whale's mouth.
The patio is swept of laurel and pine.

Now we can swim.

Mike is grinning toothily
holding the tail of an inflatable dolphin.
Nick surfaces, one eye squinting
brown hair flopped across his forehead.
I am swimming towards them
wearing a flannelette candy-striped cossie;
all-in-one with collar and shorts.

We play-fight with the dolphin as weapon
our faces pulled open
like treasure boxes.
The perfect mixture of fear and fun.

Our potential is phenomenal.
The sparkling scent of chlorine
has cleansed our skins
and we've caught the sunshine all to ourselves.

Bambi

Granddad's garage.
No motor, all workshop:
vices, chisels, hammers.
Boys-stuff.
Mickey, Bambi, Minnie, Goofy
painted on the double doors.

Backs turned to their beaming faces
Granddad and Nick
plane wood into armless soldiers
making windmills.

Golden spirals hop off the workbench
like Thumper.
Woodchips flutter like bluebirds
in sunbeams around their feet.

Working in silence together
amid echoes in the wood
legacies pass down
like rings in trees.

Granddad follows a scent
of freshly pressed ham and scones
I need a wash before my tea.

Leaving his carpenter grandson
cosy in concentration
legs splayed like Bambi

in a world of orphan infantry
conscripted to swipe and spin
do battle with the wind.

THE NAME GUESSING GAME

Every morning
whilst getting ready for school:
packing our lunch boxes
filling plastic flasks with squash
I would make my brothers play
the name guessing game.

Guess who I am today?
I'd squeal, like Rumplestiltskin.
Whoever guesses my name correctly
gets to be my favourite brother

and the names were never simple
like Anna or Emma
more Russian Chekhov-type inventions
like Pasha, Masha and Sasha.

Nick and Mike got good at guessing
humoured me
loved me
and my ability to re-invent myself
day after day after day.

DADDY
for Robert

Daddy, last week I finished a story
about a cable car disaster
only to see 'Hanging by a Thread' on TV.

You laugh at me
while I try to figure out
how the producers stole my idea
and managed to make a movie
in a week.

Excitedly, you show me a book
The Young Visitors by Daisy Ashford.
She wrote this novel when she was nine
which means she has already
beaten me to it.

You are trying to be an inspiration
and all I feel is disappointing.

I don't understand
why I'm fiercely competitive
why it's not okay to be runner-up
and why
all the time we're talking

Mummy is practising high kicks and calling
Daddy, look at me! Look at me!

THE UNANSWERABLE QUESTION

As kids
we used to laugh at this television programme
where a boy had a nightmare
about trying to answer impossible questions:

How long is a piece of string?
How many sailors on a ship?
How many pigeons in a pie?
How many trees in a wood?

We used to taunt each other
with similar conundrums
stare into each other's eyes
like inquisitors
and laugh uncontrollably
like we might shake ourselves apart.

Why did unanswerable questions
make our bodies convulse so?

I don't know. I don't know.

The Games We Play

The games we play
hurt.

Mercy: we twist our fingers
until someone breaks the painful silence.

Chinese burns: leaving red-ribbed wrists
like prisoners of war.

Logan: where knuckles are rapped
into one another's skulls.

In the garden we play catch with breeze blocks

and a game with no name
where we push the air
out of each other's lungs
until we faint.

Mike draws tank battles
on his maths books.

Nick sews his fingertips together
with needles and thread.

I pull the heads and legs off dollies.

AFTER MUCHOS SOMOS
We are Many, by Pablo Neruda

'All the books I read lionize dazzling hero figures, always
brimming with self-assurance. I die with envy of them; and, in
films where bullets fly on the wind, I am left in envy of the
cowboys, left admiring even their horses.'

For a year we lived in Sweden,
where the sun on the snow gave us tans in Winter
and the fishy-shaped salt liquorice
contorted our lips like herrings.

Daily, Nick would come home
an hour late from school
chewing over different excuses
I was chased up a tree by a giant swordfish.
An arctic fox kept me captive in its cave.

My parents gave up looking for the real answers.
For Nick was a fox himself.
A Spanish one.

His weight swaying on his back leg
left hand clenched high
pulling the bit against the foaming mouth
of his rearing black steed
while his right hand
slashed out a red zed with his sword.

Caped and masked
head looped with a wide brimmed hat
silhouetted against Stockholm's powdery sky
the mysterious hero
who couldn't safely tell the truth
about where he'd been or what he'd seen.

BUBBLES

I bathe in bubbles
while a row rages
between Mummy and Daddy.

Fee fie fo fum

I try to blot out the sounds
by blowing caves and castles
into crackling foam

until Mummy bolts in
kneels on the mat
snatches the sponge
scrubs my back
with angry hands
while I wince
in my fairyland.

Daddy thumps on the locked door
as if stoning a landed salmon
cracks the mirror damp-side
into five fractions of ceiling.

Mummy freaks
plunges my neck to knees
beyond flexibility.
Agony.
Makes a mermaid of me.

We listen to Daddy
pack his monster suitcase
and leave.

Mummy's reflection weeps
in a triangle on the floor.

I shiver
as my magic kingdom
collapses.

A fin of pain rips down my back.
For days my body curves.

Fee fie fo fum

Daddy returns
offering a replacement mirror
that promises to change wrongs to rights.
Tougher than the last.

Miraculously, my spine finds the geometry
to straighten
and I help him fix
all our trembling bodies
back up against the bathroom door.

Rosettes I
for Nick

August was yours.
Leo birthday for a lion-hearted boy.
A week at Pony Camp.

The straw at its sweetest, lightest.
The gravel a desiccated desert.

You worked single-handed.
Your determination admired
by gangly girls on horseback
pert in jodhpurs and shirts.

You made the music of rake on pebbles
to scrape every strand of gold from the yard's face
restore its complexion
in time for Sunday's gymkhana.

We siblings chose two ponies to enter the games:
Chum and Choosy
the most skittish pair on the stable block.

I entered Choosy in the show-jumping
dreaming that somehow
my worship of her skewbald colours
would make me an accomplished equestrian.

As we cat-leapt through fences
reality smacked me in the mouth.
The crowd gasped
at my bleeding lip
while I hugged Choosy's ginger mane
to stop myself going topsy-turvy
humiliated in a ring of harlequin-coloured jumps.
A joke.
Disqualified.

You and Chum
sailed over the poles
living my dream

in scraggy jeans and fitted T.

We knew you were the champ.

Two clear rounds.
Two silky rosettes
purple and yellow
purple and pink.
Perfect.

Back in the radiant yard
we watered our horses.
I snivelled the taste of blood and hot leather
mixed with sweat on Choosy's neck.
While you righted my disappointment
by offering me the purple and pink
saying I could tell Mummy and Daddy I'd won it
and the colours were too girly for you anyway.

Our secret
pinned close to my chest.
I'd keep it.

Singing Our Hearts Out

We are choristers
at Warfield Parish Church

I am in love with Susan Baker.
She is tall, blonde, beautiful
and sings like an angel.

Nick is in love with Susan Baker
but in his starched ruff
and oversized cassock
I don't think he has it.

Mike is in love with Susan Baker.
He has the best chance of all of us.
But he can't ask her out
because his time is not his own.
Even when he arrives home early
Mummy says he's late.

So how can he snatch five minutes
to sit next to Susan
on a gravestone half-hidden in the wheat-like grass?
How can he ask
for more than a smile
as she walks past?

MIKE

You are watching
responsible.

Yours and your father's baby photos
are interchangeable.

He is never available.

You are watching
responsible.

TAKING THE HEAT OFF

I'm such a smart daughter.
I've been told
how I've got more brains
than both my brothers put together.

So when Mike is in hot water
I set to work
on his behalf
as if solving algebra.

How can he permanently
take the heat off?

An equation of inverse proportion
reducing body temperature
until it becomes infinitesimal.

I've got it. I shout.
Draw a bath of water.
Lie in it.
Swallow paracetemol.
Take a knife and slice
each wrist vertically
close your eyes
count to sixty.
Chill.

I'm such a smart daughter
overflowing with formulas and theories.
But no one listens
no one listens to me.

POINTING

Nick has been locked out of the house.
He's stalking the garden like a jaguar
casting no shadow or silhouette
against the jungle of night.
He prowls, pacing, contemplating.

There has been an argument
strapping with a belt
banishment.

I am at the sink
washing-up
something's not fair
but I can't work it out

so I go far away
in a fantasy of being a dancer
pirouetting on tippy-toes
like walking on eggshells.

I look into the window
see my image
hard-boiled, purple rings for eyes.
Not much of a prima-ballerina.

There is a punch
a huge paw
hits me square on the reflected jaw.
My likeness shatters into Nick's wounded fist.

He is holding up a different mirror
one made of fury
for everyone to see the butchery
disintegration of family.

It reflects a Medusa head
which hisses
See!
The snakes point their feathery tongues
See! He's pure madness and misery.

BONE IDLE

Being driven
through London
I stare at the elegant houses
in through sash windows
and imagine my future
sitting, writing in one of them.
I already know
it will be chilly, always Autumn
the glass misted with condensation.

Today, Mike is being taken
to the psychiatrist
to find out what's wrong with him.
To find out
why he's not doing his homework
and tells stories
about not doing his homework.

He is in the psychiatrist's office.
We sit waiting for ages.
I feel the quiet in me breeding
like the inside shell of an unanswerable question
you never know what's inside
until it's broken.

On the way home it has grown dark.
The diagnosis is given
amongst shrieks of hysteria from Mummy.

Bone Idle!
a professional label for provocation.

Bone Idle
That's what you are!

And the car is full
of hideous laughter
family
silence.

'What you don't know…'

LEAVING (BETTY)

In order to go through
with some decisions
you have to divorce
body from soul.

The car is stacked
with all I'm taking
a hotchpotch of sentimentals and essentials
as if for some jolly family holiday.

Robert, my husband, is in the front room
strumming his Spanish guitar
far away from Edinburgh.

A love song.

If I didn't need him
to say *Yes*
I'd ask, *Are you playing that song for me?*

THE NIGHT THEY CAME (ALICE)

Claire arrived as a newborn does
skinny in a blanket.
You'd never guess she was a year old.

Rat-face
thumb chewed to the bone
crying constantly
except when I held her
she stopped and stared.

Turquoise eyes.
Hello.
Mousey smile.

She was saved by being a babe.
The boys' teeth were rotten
too many 'treats'.
Noisy boys
running wild.

I'm to be their new mother.
Too shattered to understand in one evening
but I do know I'll show Betty, his ex
what a mother should be:
decent food, boundaries, nurture.

We'll soon see
soon see who's best.

DOGGED (BETTY)

I feel like a clapped-out sniffer-hound
trying to pick up any whiff of information
about my children.

I think about them constantly

I lie out flat on top of the bedspread
and stare at the ceiling.
That's when I see them.
Nick running towards me
leaning into the wind with aeroplane arms.
Mike in his *Gadabout* car
wearing that blue crash helmet
so much like his dad.
He's probably grown too big for it now.
Claire will be walking and talking.

Do they call his new wife *Mummy?*

I went to visit my ex-mother-in-law.
She hasn't seen her grandchildren for two years.
But still, she had a few scraps for me.
The boys had skateboards for Christmas
hand-made by their dad.
Nick seems bright.
Claire is bonny.
I wonder if she looks like me?

People treat me like I never had kids.
Sometimes, I'm buying cigarettes in the newsagent
and I want to scream *I gave birth to three children!*

Even close friends don't mention them.
They look at me with pansy eyes
like I'm an old pet they are fond of

but is dying of some dreadful disease
like they're killing time
before the vet comes round
to put me out of my misery.

The Silver Tassie (Robert)

I am in Scotland on business
and make a sneaky visit to Lochgelly
where I'll ask after Betty
at her brother's pub, The Silver Tassie.

Jim looks shocked to see me.
It has been two years
since my last enquiry
How is she? I ask.

Get a firm reply
bunch of five
straight between the eyes.

THE LEGACY (ALICE)

I have to say I was grateful.
We could get on with being a family:
the kids, Robert and me.
Some days I'd forget
she existed

and then Claire would come home
wearing a sneer
saying a present I'd given her
wasn't big enough
and I'd feel Betty was here
in the house even.

The battle-lines have been redrawn.
She's gone

yet strangely, taken on a more sinister
phantom form
an undefeatable adversary
who can see straight through me.

I glimpse shadows where there aren't any.
Trouble sleeping.

What a cruel legacy
to leave three children.

THE BLACK EYE (ROBERT)

'No one kills himself who has not wanted to kill another.'
from The Savage God, by Al Alvarez.

After the black eyes subsided
another swelled inside me.

Bruised tissue
I bashed over again

so the lid never healed
so the flesh never peeled
so the eye could not see

only feel
the seeping of its savage blindness.

ALICE IN WONDERLAND (ALICE)

I told my friends
how I fancied fairy tales never happened
then found myself in the middle of one.

It began as a dream
winning the man I loved
complete with the family
I could never bear from my body.
I was delighted
like winning a game of chess
when you've lost your queen.

Your mind plays strange tricks
in reverie.
The children I'd cradled in my arms
turned out to be piglets.
A practical joke.
Their stench turned my stomach
but I nursed them anyway.

My husband tutored me in ways of discipline
I learned them well through their delivery
how say-so can shrink you down
until you feel you might extinguish
like a candle.

But I'm a smart girl.
I learned how to grow like an inferno
so large, I filled the whole house
from chimneys to windows
self-defence against the annihilation
of me.

When I grew
I watched those piglets
and even my husband reduce in size and crackle.

In those moments
I wasn't sure what I was doing
except it was choking everything.

My silence was golden.
I couldn't speak
about how difficult it was to breathe
when you're watched so carefully.
My every movement measured
in grunts and squeals.
I couldn't say *This isn't me.*
This isn't the way it was meant to be.

I watched the piglets struggle and plummet
from my arms
trot away
without a backward glance.

They forgot that I'd held them.
Only remembered, I'd dropped them.

And when I woke up
I looked at the lines in my skin
and they were deep
but empty.

So much time had passed
and I had nothing to show
for my sacrifice.

ARTIFICIAL INTELLIGENCE (ROBERT)

I sit at my computer, elbows on the keyboard
hands covering my mouth

don't have to reply
to the silent screen, screaming.

I create a virtual world
with games. *Let's play!*

I can program programmes
to learn by themselves

everything written in code.
I speak several symbolic languages.

Bad language too.
I get angry, fucking furious.

So would you
carrying this bruise.

For all my qualifications
I can't get life to add up

not to anything more than bloody disaster.
And I certainly don't have the words.

I like things clear-cut, black-white like barcode
one-zero like binary.

This pulse
on off.

This secret
in out.

No fuzzy logic.
Grey matter.

LETTING THE CAT OUT OF THE BAG (ALICE)

It is my birthday.
We have decided today is the day
to let the cat out of the bag.

I put on my purple velvet dressing gown
with the dragon fastening.
It's Claire's favourite.
She likes to unclip and re-clip the buckle
dissecting the dragon
looking at half of it
the non-dragon
then making it whole again.
But today feels like vivisection.

Robert calls her in for me.
As soon as she appears
I can't hold back the tears.
Her long blonde hair pinned back at the sides.
A young twelve
and I'm about to change her world.
I savour the last moments
of the way things are.
Wish I could stop her from growing
older, wiser.

Mummy, why are you crying?
I get her to sit down beside me
on the sofa.
I hold her hand
but really, she's holding mine.

I've rehearsed the words a thousand times
Would it matter
if I didn't hold you in my tummy for nine months?
Her face crumples like a collapsing lung
not in upset, but a question.

She doesn't comprehend.

I reassure her
I am your real Mummy
but Daddy was married before
and you and the boys
are from his first marriage.

Claire looks at Robert
You were married before?

Yes, he says.
She looks disgusted.
I say, *Do you want to ask any questions?*

What happened to Daddy's first wife?
She's as sharp as a knife.

I take a deep breath
wondering how little I can get away
with giving away.
Her name was Betty
and I'm afraid she died.

I feel like a murderer.
Claire looks past both of us
out into the garden
passively watching the neighbour's cat
trespass across the patio.

I want to get inside her
see what she's thinking.
I need to know she's not split open.
The way I feel.
She must hate me.
Hate us
for this secret.

Can we get on with your birthday, now?
She says, all madam, matter of fact
still herself, still whole
and goes out to get her gift for me.

I look at Robert.
I'm disgusted too
to be part of this experiment.
The half truth.

Blackbird Hall

MOVING

Looking back
it came after a series of catastrophes.

The neighbours had called the police
after seeing Mum chasing Mike
with a pitchfork around the garden.

Nick had gone running to a family friend
saying, *Please protect me.*

A boy at school teased me
about having psycho parents.

So we moved towns
and somewhere along the way
we mislaid my brothers.

When we unpacked
their things had vanished.
There was nothing

nothing of theirs
and the extra rooms
became offices
in a secluded mansion
at the end
of a long, long drive.

LONDON ZOO

Summer's afternoon
Dad drove from the Greek restaurant
towards London Zoo.

I knew the rest of the day
was balanced like a crouching cheetah.

Mum said: *I'm not sure if there is time for the zoo.*

It was supposed to be a treat for me.
I begged *Please let's go.*
There are baby elephants
(they were her favourites).

She relented.
The day relaxed.
Sun strobed through hazy traffic and capital bustle
like running past a cage.

I got a little out of my mind
on victory, excitement.

We arrived at the zoo.
Mum quibbled about the cost
but Dad paid our way in
under an animal studded canopy.

I said I needed the loo.
Mum sighed: *I don't believe it.*
Why didn't you go in the restaurant?

I didn't need to go then.
She grumped off in a huff
head in her hands
trapped as the chimps
which hooted and shrieked.

Dad followed Mum
I watched them gesticulate
exchange bad language.

I sneaked away to the toilet.

It only took a minute.

When I returned
Dad grabbed me by the scruff
marched me back outside the gates
into the street
slapped my cheek with orang-utan hands.
I felt my head may have left my neck
for a flash.

There was a sense of tableau.
London stopped to look.

One man unfroze
confronted my father.

They faced up like a pair of kangaroos.
My Dad's strangled Scots accent
wrenched at the stranger's throat.

Stop! I screamed.
The man lost his voice
rejoined the crowd.

I was dragged sniffling
back underneath the canopy.
Reconciliation with Mum.
Shaky apology from me.

We made 'happy families'
looked around the animals.

I don't recall any of them.
Just faces staring

and mine burning.

A FISTFUL OF FLOWERS

I always think of the line
Mrs Dalloway said she would buy the flowers herself

because I wish Mum had.

It was only when I mentioned
I had chosen them at lunch
that she imagined they'd wilted

punched me in the street with gardener's fists
hard enough to halt a passer-by

rosy cheeked
hare's tail locks
lemon blouse
fresh as daffodils
Are you alright?

I told her to *Piss-off.*
I didn't mean it.
I meant *Rescue me, please.*

Mum sent me penniless to the florist
who, with my tear-smacked face I terrorised
into surrendering replacement lilies.
A triumph of trembling.

But Mum was still furious
told me how ashamed she felt
to hand that magnificent bouquet to her friend.

Wiping the Slate Clean

I know there is a debt.
Although I don't know quite how it came about
but I believe I can pay it off
in chores.

I sweep the dogs' room
empty the bins
clean the oven
and the hob
empty the dishwasher
lay the table
vacuum the bedrooms
empty the bins
rake the lawn
polish the silver
clean out the cupboards
beeswax the marble
empty the bins
wash the gate
weed the borders
tidy the garage
mop the kitchen
buff the cutlery
empty the bins
clean my parents' clean golf shoes.

I clean and clean and clean and clean
but however much effort I make
how tired I am
or how raw my hands

I can't seem
to wipe that slate.

DOMESTICITY

Saturday isn't the customary day
for aggression.
Mum normally exercises it
on a school day
between my home-time and Dad's.

So today it's an extra helping in the kitchen
my blood drips
onto the bronzed herringbone of the tiles
from my nose.

That floor was clean she shrieks.
I instinctively tilt my head back, sniff
and use my hand to block the flow
pushing it up across my cheeks
like war-paint

Dad's footsteps wallop down the stairs
What the hell's going on here?

I feel him draw near
deep breathing
I smell him.
But all I can see
is the hint-of-barley ceiling.

You've gone too far, this time! He shouts
and I look down
with a surge of scarlet snot.

He thinks she's cut my face.
He's got her cornered.
It's only a nosebleed I protest.
He backs off.
Relieved.

And I am pleased
to hear *too far*
and be passed a tissue.

ALL ABOUT MY MOTHER
for Robert

You only mentioned her once
pointing out a waitress in a restaurant
That woman is the spitting image of your mother.

Alice closed you down
a snap slipped across the table with the salt.

For the rest of the meal
we dined on an air of shame, tension
indigestion.

The only other time
you uttered her name
I brought her up from the depths of my guts

an almost involuntary vomit
of curiosity
What was Betty like?

Your face said something subtle
about sinews and flesh.

It felt like you were ruminating
towards a black hole I couldn't even imagine
She was confused and unhappy.

I have the feeling
you said you didn't
want to talk about it.

I have the feeling you didn't
say anything.

But something to do with the angle
of your elbow to the table
told me
ça suffit.

WOULDN'T YOU JUST DIE WITHOUT MAHLER?
title from the film 'Educating Rita' by Willy Russell

Father, whenever I think of you
you are on your way out
pack-lunch tucked in your bag like a schoolboy
kisses from Mum
then off to work.

Always disappearing
through some doorway
to urgently mow the lawn;
work on a software problem.

Sometimes you stayed up all night
and I don't blame you.
Peace and quiet.

Your exquisite brain
moving like clockwork to Mahler.

Don't think I didn't hear you.
I stayed awake too
wondering what on earth I could do.

What I could change about myself
to make this brilliant man
spend more time with me.

So I studied hard, harder, hardest
in the hope one day I'd be
your contemporary.

The Other Half

We are in a different house
but on the same sofa
where I discovered
my mother was not my birth mother.

My father is missing two packets of beta-blockers.
The finger immediately points to me.
This time they are spot-on.
Bingo!
I want them to know.

I ate them all like Smarties
hounding Monday to Sunday round and round
two weeks worth in an afternoon
like a greedy pig.
If they hadn't tasted bitter
they would have been delicious.

I'd hoped what could steady the heart in one dose
would still the heart in overdose.
I was wrong.

It is time
my step-mother says
to let me know
how my birth-mother died.
It was suicide.

She stares at me accusingly
I'm guilty of the same criminality
trying to injure other people
through my insatiable self-interest.

I'm never asked for a reason
to justify my actions.

The verdict announced
attention-seeking.

I'm forgiven.

I'm forgotten.

Leaving Home

I take my boxer dogs for a long hike.
They have to be walked individually.
Two together is too much for me.

Once they dragged me
all the way down the sandy lane
on my front
and across the road at the bottom
to attack a lurcher.
I'll never forget how the fear
stiffened its owner's face
tightened by my screams
as if he'd seen the very hounds of hell approach.
I imagine this scene
stole years from him.

But today is different.
I am silent and the walks are special.
I take each dog their favourite route.
Try to make the journeys equal
so they can smell each other on the hedgerows.

The overgrown churchyard
is misted in pollen.
The grass darts stand tall
independent.
The graves have always had their peace
but somehow seem settled, deeper.
I notice the moss and the lichen
are both green, yet dissimilar.

Walking back up the drive, I'm terrified.
I've never left home before.

There is a note in my step-mother's handwriting.
Your father has been rushed to hospital.
You can take a taxi if you choose.

I choose.

The driver looks bemused
yet strangely moved
as he helps me load
sixteen carrier bags of possessions
into his panting diesel.

He says nothing
in reply to my snivels.

We steer up the drive
Blackbird Hall shrinks.

My dogs compete
to press their farewell noses
hard up against the conservatory door.

Searching

WICKED STEP-MOTHER
for Alice

You are the wicked step-mother.
I am Hansel and Gretel
led out to the forest by your husband and dumped.

You are the wicked step-mother.
I am Snow White
my blood blushes the blizzard.

You are the wicked step-mother.
I am Cinderella.
You will not let me go to the ball
in case I turn out to be
the fairest of them all.

You are the wicked step-mother.
I am the child
trapped in a story
where all we can be
is in rivalry

even though I know
you want to hug me
hold me
keep me
your stolen baby
forever
live happily ever after
together.

I need to find my way out of the forest.
Go to the ball.
Turn into a woman.
Ignore your calls.

WOMANKIND

The counsellor is gentle
I like her.
She tells me to stop telling her stories.

She means my life tied up
in neat little packages
like poetry.

It's beyond me

so I tell her one of my tales
about the twin
who hates her sister
because she can never be separate
until her twin dies
and that's when she knows
how much she loved her.

That's your step-mother she says.
You're still tangled up in her.
You can't be yourself
because you can't let go.

I'm my own poem.
Mummified in narrative.

It saved my life
and now I'm lost in the funhouse.

That's time! She says
and after months of wandering in a whiteout of words
I finally notice the door.

Are you Ready?
for Nicola

We are standing
outside the central library
on Bristol's College Green
where skaters stunt around us
in a frenzy of risk-taking.

Are you ready to do this? She asks.
I've known her a year.
Long enough to notice
that the skin on her face
is always baby smooth
and the glitter cosmetic
dotted under her eyes
is symbolic of suffering.

She is helping me search
for my birth-mother's family.

One step at a time.
Today the first.
Her death certificate.

I'm not ready
for a new perspective
desiring and resisting
in equal measures.
The stretch inside me
strains my silent chest.

Inside the library's wooden body
I fear this journey
may take me away from cosy fantasies
of the perfect mother.

Upstairs, the 'Births, Deaths and Marriages' records
are panting, swallowing all the oxygen.
I feel panicked, claustrophobic.

Where is Scotland?

Nicola asks the question on my behalf
because my voice has been strangled.

Scotland? No, it's not here.
We only stock England.
You have to go to Scotland for Scotland.

Back outside I'm still struggling to breathe
Nicola says
I'm sorry.

But it's not her fault
that I'm in the wrong country.

I want to scream
blow my celtic horn
but I don't possess one.

Instead I catch my breath
enough to share a sandwich
and pieces of each other.

We talk looking forward
watch the skaters
turn the ball bearings
that move the wheels
that help them fly
that threaten their lives.

Diary on Amalfi Beach

I am a house
built on sand
my foundations constructed on questions
and half-truths.
It is only a matter of time
before the tide turns and takes me with it.

I shall search for my birth mother's family
even if it sends an earthquake to swallow me
I cannot live in the land of not-knowing forever.
The shores are shrinking
soon to be a wisp of gold, like a strand of my hair.
The rocks are leering.
It gets cold by noon in their red shadow.

I long to touch something my mother touched.
Just to see a photo of her and know some likeness
would feel like bathing in lava
it should turn the sand to glass at least.

FINGERS CROSSED

Sudeley Castle will always have a special place in history
neglected for two hundred years
then rebuilt lovingly
by the glove-making Dent family
who knew about hands
and how to keep them warm, elegant.

My hands are always cold
even in high Summer
as I press the phone
against my face
in a Tudor knot garden
to receive an unexpected call
from the Family Tracing Service.

They have found my uncle.

There are living blood ties with my fingers
which have been crossed so long.

A chance for restoration
to build a house of stone
and conceivably
a castle.

THE GEESE ARE HEADING HOME
for Isabel Johnstone
(After 'Wild Geese', by Mary Oliver)

Before I opened it
I held the packet
postmarked Edinburgh
for ages in my trembling hands.

I felt the swaddling of the envelope
with an airborne thrill in my stomach.

I knew the pictures
of my birth-mother, Betty
were inside.

When I was ready
I slid my finger into the package's cotton mouth.

I read your letter first.
A profound side of typed A4
ending with your emotions
getting the better of you.
Me too.

The photos lay snug in their own downy vest
aromatic with tobacco.

I unwrapped them
like fledglings bound in velvet
and there was my mother
at Edinburgh Zoo
sitting on the grass
wearing off-white pumps and a blue jacket.
Mike unmistakeable
next to her
in a push chair.

I stared for ages
at her face, her hair.

I stared in the mirror

compared her to me.

More letters followed
like a flock of swallows arriving
with your chirping accent in my mind

then the tone slowed
as you prepared me for the details
of my mother's death.

You have rewound this story
many times in your head already.
You tell me tentatively, tenderly

how she was found by her mother
on the sofa
with a brown smudge
around her mouth
alive, lucid
had a conversation
about the staining
plant-poison potion.
Paraquat.
Why did she drink that?

Ambulance.
Hospital.
Hope.

But you cannot drink paraquat and survive.
Early the next morning, she died.

The postman
our carrier-pigeon
faithfully continues
to drop your letters through my door.

I learn that self-destruction
is no stranger to your family.

Your sister, Davina
a box of ashes on your lap

as you took a train back from Manchester.
I imagine you gazed out the window
noticed the starlings nesting in the burnished hedgerows.

Ahead of our rendezvous
you write simply of wild geese
going wherever they go

calling out to you and me
on their long journeys home.

THE WELCOME PARTY

We are lucky to fly.
Make the ascent
through gale force winds.
I'm obtuse, say to Mike
I've waited twenty-nine years
for this meeting and I'm not waiting another day.
He finds my impatience entertaining.

At Edinburgh arrivals
a plethora of hugs
and expressions.
A welcome party.

No chance
to top up my lippy
prepare a face for the reunion
so I wear this one

to meet the faces of my family
I don't recognise
but they recognise me.
You look a lot like Betty.

I receive some of her jewellery:
earrings, necklace, watch
and a family photo album
that requires explanation.
Shows the workings out
behind the sum of three.

My first ever baby pictures
me, a blue-eyed bundle
held by both my brothers.

I wish Nick was here
just split up with his girlfriend.
In no fit state, but there's plenty of time.

I began with a name: James, my Uncle Jim
and he has multiplied

into three beautiful daughters
who have squared into
nine beautiful grandchildren.

Three each.
Fair's fair.

I wonder what it would have been like
to grow up around so much family

another dimension
go back in time
to a different decision.

It doesn't bear calculating
I've found what I didn't lose
and I'm celebrating.

ENOUGH
for Jim Johnstone

The day following the reunion
we went for a walk around Loch Ore
to clear our heads.

You pulled away from the family band
the dog, an excuse

while we chattered behind
exhaling memories
visible in the cold air.

Fisherman wader-deep in water
on a mobile-phone arrests our attention.

You return with the news:
Body in the lake
man aged eaty-three
he couldnee taek anymoor.

I picture his inflated dinghy-skin
stretched to capacity
tartan slippers thistling

flannel trousers swathing grey flesh, muscle, bone.
His face an underwater moon

yours composed
although being dragged backwards
to twenty-two years ago
where the undercurrents
still pull deep down

deep down below.

SEAFIELD CREMATORIUM

We thin out towards the garden of remembrance
brush past a coffin perched on four shoulders.
It is entering the incinerator.
Veneered chipboard soon to be ash.

We weed plastic plaques with our eyes, rejecting names:
MacFarlane, Kilpatrick, Lockhart
embedded by roses:
Red Masquerade, Balkan Star, Remembrance.

Raking over the past
seems vicious now.
Grief turns over
like mounds of turf
leaving my family's raw underbelly exposed.

I've been here before.
I know there is no marker.

My memorial is always with me:
mannerisms, laugh, blood
and dug into my marrowbone
her name, Betty Johnstone.

LONG DISTANCE LOVE
for Aunt Muriel

I was lost to you for a long time.

Your daughter reported
how when your sister died
you hugged your husband on the bed
and cried together
mourning far away in Canada.

Twenty-three years later
it is Valentines
and you have sent your niece a present
all this way.

I sit in the car park
of the Royal Mail collection office
and play pass the parcel with myself
and all the delicate layers
of exquisite tissue paper.

It is Valentines
and my heart is being unwrapped
with a tug of its purple ribbon fastening
unfolding like a petal bundle
fluttering in my hands.

WORCESTER
for my cousin, Maureen

We meet, just us, for the first time
in Worcester Museum's café.

I could have dreamed this place:
rectangular marbled gallery space
above the grand entrance
creating a vortex of voices
in the midst of granite columns
fanning palms
text along the cornice
like I like it

all guarding the entrance
to fine art, archaeology, ancestry,
but that's not what we came here to see.

You paint me a picture of Betty, my mother:
party girl, persuasive
damaged by divorce
turned to drink, then suicide.

You brush the dust
from my dated understanding
by creating a landscape:
the Buxton hotel where she worked;
her reluctant return to Edinburgh.

You help me to build
a family tree sprouting with blood lines.

Towards the end of our meeting
you say something
about how Robert and Alice
must have looked at me daily
and seen Betty

and I remember words scribbled
on the first crisp page
of a teenage diary:

New Years Day '88
Today, Mummy said:
'I want to smash your face until its unrecognisable.'

And that is when I notice
the triangle
not of love
but of fear

a magnetic hole
that could suck us all hollow as this hall

that we are now leaving
hugging goodbye.

I'm driving home alone
but not yet ready to go
climb two-hundred-and-thirty-five steps
to the top of Worcester Cathedral
and after a claustrophobic, shadowy ascendance
suddenly I emerge high
able to see for miles and miles.

DELEGATION
for Betty

Now, it seems you remind me
of a colleague who goes on holiday
and leaves me with her workload
in files named:
anxiety, fear, guilt and shame

and just when I think
I might be getting to grips with it again
I remember that she has also

handed in her notice.

THE MOTHER-MOTHER TREE

I may have looked whole
beautiful from the outside
With all those looks and talents
why wasn't she more successful?

But inside
I was like one of those trees
split down the trunk
by a bolt of lightening

still growing
but in two pieces
arching apart

bound around with bandages and tar
pulling myself together
on a daily basis
grasping the wood-wormed guts
that I am too horrified to show you.

All my rings are broken.
They will never add up to anything I'll understand
never mind anyone else.

I will be married
and desperately disenchanted
because I put love
below security

and I can't love
somebody fully
when I'm half and half.
Just like my birth-mother before me
I will depart.

But it gets easier
when I strip off the bark
and try not to feel ashamed
or responsible for more than myself.

Maturing, knowing that every gnarl and crook
is part of me.

Learning
how to hold somebody else.

Concentrating on the sky
not the scars.

In my tallest branches
I can now hold
both Venus and Mars.

BROTHER

Nick

When I Heard the News

I was in the city centre
a cellophaned January day.
Crinkled light deflected from Pero's bridge
built in memory of Africans
who suffered in the triangle of trade.

I couldn't believe
how it didn't lose its pride
to the information of Nick's suicide.

Two enormous horns
curved like courting swans upon the water.

But it is still walked all over.
A fate captured in its architecture.

Slaves
like my brother
forced by his parents
to crawl on hands and knees
branded too animal to stand upright

couldn't shake the labels:
dirty, lazy, scum

shifted from field to field
picked fruit, hops, daffodils.
Black beneath his fingernails.

Always scape-goated against the fence
of the civilised.

Home
the shoes on his feet

rather jump ship
than live with a victim's stench.

Pero's bridge arched defiant
shrink-wrapped remembrance.

When I heard the news
its horns cried
freedom
freedom.

Stari Most (Old Bridge – Mostar, Bosnia)
for Nick

*'The Old Bridge was more than a thing of striking beauty. "A
crescent moon in stone" a Muslim poet once called it. Linking
Croats, Serbs, Muslims and others who lived on the two sides of
the river, the bridge came to symbolize the mix of peoples in the
old Yugoslavia who lived side by side before war and ethnic
hatred shattered their country in the early 1990s. When
Croatian artillery shells sent it crashing into the Neretva River,
the shock waves travelled far and wide.'*

Stari Most
began to haunt me
followed me into
newspapers, magazines, radio.
It was even in the air I breathed.

Ask me what it is
and I'll say.
It isn't.
That's just it.
Like you
it's not there.

It hung perfectly in its last few moments
suddenly alive
then collapsed

an amputated arm
with a phantom existence.

I still feel your pain
with a reality so strong
I can even sense you touch my face.
At times I reach out
only to confront
the absence.

That non-bridge
binds Mostar together
in an impossible hug

a symbol of understanding
reminiscent of the days
when all the towns varied cultures
lived side by side like brothers.

II

They are building the bridge again.
Hauling stone from the River Neretva.
Chunks weighing up to ninety tonnes.
Divers risk their lives
in the underworld to bring it back.

Demirovic
the man commanding the resurrection
has faith, says *God likes passionate people.*

I admire his conviction
but my passion
cannot rebuild the physical.
I hold my breath like a prayer
but I'm not going under.

An Empty Catkin
for Nick

An empty catkin
has shed all its golden pollen
given everything up
like a good boy.

Its brown casing
the way it spins down in staves

has a twist of DNA about it.
Its destiny decided
long before it caterpillared
from weeping willow.

And yet it has
a backbone quality
each vertebra separated
by discarded delicate tissue.
Bend it the wrong way
and it will surely

snap.

I think of your spine
longer than ever
first and last time
hanging in the outbuilding air.

Waiting for a friend
to take your weight
your six foot of muscle and bone
and curiously disconnect you
from your branch.

RIDE ON I

Christy Moore's song 'Ride On' was chosen by Mike
Williamson to play at Nick's cremation.

Even though his sister was horse-mad
it was Nick who had a way with them.
Horse-whisperer before his time
he'd commune with the most brutal of beasts.
Muddy face hard up against a bay muzzle
short hairs bristling his nose
they'd sway together like tribesmen.

He was a horse-man.
He knew what it was to be broken-in.
Strong back capable of carrying bundles of burdens.
Long neck and a proud face in repose.
His laugh, a whinny.
Mounted
two became one.

Never cruel
he knew the laws of nature
its okay to kill a rabbit
if you hunt it like a man
use a bow and arrow
skin it
cook it
eat it.

He was as hard as the steed
in *Gone with the Wind*.
Yet as green as a colt
when love came calling.
Nick would have offered
to carry Scarlett O'Hara
all the way to Tara
and let her whip him to the ground
when he got there.

He wasn't born to be tamed.
Resisted it with every sinew
wild to the heart

with fighting to live freely from the terrain.
Stubborn.

To the last
he craved the company of horses.
When he went missing
they thought maybe he'd been riding the gypsy ponies bareback
fallen off and cracked his head.

Instead, he'd found a tether rope
woven with wrath.
If Nick was going to be restrained
he'd rather tie the knot himself.

His last ride
taken solo.
Purple clouds moving west
against a cider twilight.

That night
he saddled the most brutish of them all.

Haiku

moss for memory
soft velcro hooks to damp earth
hold not too tightly

WEST HOPE
for Nicola

I

You are the chosen one
above my brother, husband
any other friend.

Because this mission
requires a person of experience.
A wounded heroine.

II

You offer to drive.
You're probably right
but I know I've got to hold on
to something.

We have a rendezvous at the Little Chef outside Leominster
with Gill from Dawe Brothers Funeral Directors.
She has Nick's ashes in an oak box.
Our trip is futile without her Saturday generosity
and we are late.

I see the wooded hill described in Gill's directions.
We just have to get the other side and we'll be there.
It feels like it's moving
Fear not, till Birnam wood
Do come to Dunsinane.

No Shakespearean illusion
just grey tarmac January reality
we arrive eventually
make our strange exchange in the car park.
Nick would have laughed.
I do too
then cry over the laminated menu
and your buttered tea-cake.

III

We are on the road again
and roll-up in good time at our second destination.

As I step out of the car into the mud of the farm
I realise that your dark hair will be a foil for me.
That Nick's friends will see you as his sister first.
A moment for me to stay in shadow.

I am afraid of this courtroom of travellers
that I will be judged an inadequate sister.

IV

Acquaintances are made.
I allow myself to be seen.
There is no uprising.
We are all here for one reason.
Nick.
He is placed on the boot of a Ford Cortina
alongside a home-made wreath and bunches of wild flowers.

I gather faces and stories:
Rachel, Val, Matt, Nathan
like making a jigsaw with missing pieces.

Our feet are frozen.
You are patient beyond words.

V

The procession begins:
a hotchpotch of lorries, cars, wagons.
We journey towards West Hope
the burial site.

Sarah, Nick's girlfriend, is with us briefly
a wiggle of fuchsia coat and hair in bunches
until she remembers she's forgotten Nick's dogs:
Solar and Posh Paws.

Take three steps back.

VI

In the middle of nowhere
one lorry blows a tyre
and we witness the combination of mishap and resourcefulness
that epitomises this community.
Vehicles spread out across the lay-by
and way beyond against a cinder sky.
A fitting fold of pilgrims.

Someone says our car should lead the parade.
We prop Nick's box up in the back window
like a carry-on film.
Lead on MacDuff.

VII

I am still clutching the wheel.
You are navigating unfamiliar land.
It is somersaulting hills, turning forest
signs for selling, not steering.
We miss the turn at Craven's Arms
end up disorientated.

I'm snappy.
don't want to admit
we've gone wrong.

We turn around
exhausted
are joined by Nathan
who inherits your place next to me
a moment for you to take a back-seat
come off-duty.

He guides us through country lanes
where a thousand snowdrops
hang their delicate necks
in respect.

VIII

The final procession is made on foot.
A gaudy gaggle:
men, women, children.

Sarah and I carry Nick's box.
Posh Paws pulls at her lead.
Solar plods alongside, resigned.

Someone carries a spade.
I deduce we have to dig our own hole.

It is the hardest work on earth.
The men take turns
sweating against the chill of the dying day.

Children sit in Nick's tree
and lie on their front in the soil
wearing fairy dresses and dungarees
get their hands deep into the hole
pull out fistfuls of earth.

I am upright, stiff with sorrow.
You are being there

enduring:
tears, speeches
air thick with the scent of healing sage
and sadness.

IX

Time to trace our footsteps back up the lane.
The light is silhouetting:
church, hedgerows, horses, phone box.

We hold hands
say nothing.

There's something between us
that will never wash off.

I don't know what you're thinking
but know it has meaning
wise from your own journey
when you were crippled.

I'm listening to the invisible birdsong
thinking of nature
and what Nick will miss out on.

I trust you completely
because, like me, you know what it is
to visit the threshold of death
on your knees
and find the faith to rise
from the bloody battlefield
even though the sky is broken

and walk.

KNOCKING
for Nick

Could it really be all
about mothers and sons?

The day you received the jiffy-bag
packed with details
of our lost family
from me

your former girlfriend took the liberty
to cheat on you.

Was she your mother too?
Rendered suddenly unnecessary.

I won't ever know whether to feel accountable
for my parcel
but part of me refuses
to take responsibility
for your downward spiral.

I was the one family member
who didn't abandon you
wanted truth

kept coming knocking for you
like an old friend
found you in fields even
back then, when you were breathing

and now I hear the echoes
of my own knuckles
on your coffin.

Do you?

Haiku

my chest a conker
split by its expanding pith
grief has outgrown me

VENICE
for Nick
(Quotes from 'Peter Pan' by J.M.Barrie)

I

From the plane

'I just want always to be a little boy and have fun.'

The islands look like Neverlands.
I recognised them instantly.
They had been looking for us
since we'd spotted them
through our childhood 3D slide viewer.
Just as magnificent
floating in the mist
at thirty-one years, as at five.
We had held that deep faraway image
against our faces for so long
our eyes were as square as that slide.

II

The Bridge of Sighs

'I thought like you that my mother would always keep the
window open for me; so I stayed away for moons and moons
and moons and then flew back; but the window was barred, for
mother had forgotten all about me.'

In the Doge's Palace we cross
The Ponte de Sospiri
where condemned men
peered through lattice windows
and saw the moon in the lagoon and gasped.
Exhaled.

III

Carnivale (Farewell to meat)

'Now if Peter had ever had a mother, he no longer missed her.
He could do very well without one. He had thought them out
and remembered only their bad points.'

The carnivale is starting.
The grandest masquerade of disguise
tricks the mind
that transforms men into women
women into men
in floor-length cloaks
with papier-mâché faces
an opportunity to project your desires and needs
onto the facade of this chaotic maze:
canals, bridges, squares.
Believe whatever makes you feel better.

For a moment I have found you and Betty
in the underworld
we are all
dancing
hugging
sweeping the streets with our joy
brother sister mother son daughter.

IV

The Boy who Never Grew Up

'Next moment he was standing on the rock again, with that
smile on his face and a drum beating within him. It was saying,
"To die will be an awfully big adventure".'

It is time to cross
ponte degli scalzi
over the Grand Canal
into the *Statione San Lucia*
and go home.

I am on the bridge
crying.
I don't want to leave you and Betty
behind in Neverlands.

My legs don't work
my back feels hunched and decrepit.
I fear I will disintegrate
if I stay in this moment any longer.

My husband is pulling at my arm
and I am stamping my feet.
Why must I be trapped in this not-child, not-adult place?

Nick, you have forgotten.
And I am your memory.
You will always be
the little boy who never grew up.

V

The Return Home

'*He had ecstasies innumerable that other children can never
know; but he was looking at the one joy from which he must be
for ever barred.*'

My husband is holding my hand.
We are flying up and away
watching the sun play on plasticine water
watching Venice shrink
into distance.

It has come to this
a cold coroner's office in Hereford
with olive leather-bound blotting pads
like placemats at a dining table.

There's one spare setting
but the only meal on offer
is a feast of indigestibles.

Whilst waiting for the hors d'eouvres
the pathologist is sweet
makes small talk
about the Mappa Mundi
and Hereford's heritage.

I study his hands.
The hands that weighed and measured Nick
extracted organs
cut off his crown
only knew him in inches and pounds
ingredients of his investigations.

I've had eight months
to put together a recipe for Nick's last hours
and most of the evidence matches
my imagination
but there's a couple of unexpected items
I hadn't bargained for:

His arm fixed above his head;
Solar, his dog, below his feet.

Mike groans beside me
and I am a spilt glass of water
all over the blotting paper.

I'd envisaged a struggle.
The body versus the mind
but hadn't accounted for a change of heart.

Nick, drunk, reaching up
trying to grasp the blue cord
above the noose and wriggle out.

Solar, our missing witness
powerless in her doggy body
whining with the question, *Why?*
no inquest will ever satisfy.

You Can't Judge a Book by its Cover
for the pathologist

You are clever.
You opened up Nick
like a detective novel
and read his body

told us
if it was any consolation
there was no evidence
to suggest he had abused heroin

as if we could restore
some family pride.

I'm grateful
for the heroin
it kept him alive

as for family pride
we have all of that we need
thank you.

Pride enough
to dress-up in diamante
smile at a dinner-party

never mentioning
the son hung-up in the cloakroom.

Pride enough
to hide all the gruesome sagas inside
which I am now wise enough to read
like an illustrated edition of Grimm's Fairy Tales.

So, I appreciate the offering
but we have family pride enough.

Thank you.

WHEN THEY HEARD THE NEWS
for Nick

When you died
it was Mike who phoned them
told them their youngest son was hung dead.

They weren't surprised.
Didn't arrive.

Instead, they packaged memories in a box:
original photos of us all
your stuffed camel
and my Tricky-Woo dog.

And I wonder who took the parcel
to the post office, Mum or Dad?

Or did they both stand in the queue
washing their hands of Mike, me and you?

And when they reached
the head of the line
did they hug the box, one last time?

And what cost when they weighed and paid?
Was all that our acquaintance meant
finally totalled in pounds and pence?

The Journey

Am I Ready?

I have an airline ticket
a bag of books, photos
two rosettes, a stuffed camel
and a bow and arrow
for a boy who has lost his father.

Am I ready?
I ask myself
to make this journey

to fly
to fly as far away
from everything and everyone I have ever known
as it is possible.

Am I ready?
to abandon everybody
except me.

Rosettes II
for Jake

I have decided to take the two rosettes
purple and yellow
purple and pink
to New Zealand
when I meet you (my nephew)
for the first time.

We will sit tiny
in the towering landscape
where the Riders of Rohan
fought for Gondor
for the World of Men.

I will hold both the prizes
on my lap as I explain
how much your father loved you
and how he hoped one day
you'd turn up at his door
and punch him in the face.

I shall tell you how much he adored horses
and about the Sunday gymkhana
when he gave his cry-baby sister half his honour
even though he was always such a small-winner.

I'll tell you
how I don't remember
why I ended up with both rosettes
(I guess I'm just better at holding onto things).

I'll say:
I'm going to keep the purple and pink
(because the colours are girly anyway)
and give you the purple and yellow.

I'll tell you to hold on to it tightly
because it's a symbol
of your father's courage and generosity
which you will never see

and that I know
if he hadn't lost his battle
in the World of Men,
if he'd felt he had the power
he would have given everything up
just to hold you
tightly again.

Two Not One

'*And there, till Christ call forth the dead, In silence let him lie:*
No need to waste the foolish tear, Or heave the windy sigh: The
man had killed the thing he loved, And so he had to die.'
from The Ballad of Reading Gaol, by Oscar Wilde

At last
the answer
to the unanswerable question.

Over a year after your death
I discover how you tried to strangle your son's mother
with him inside her
and how you punched her stomach
and murdered his twin.

And I feel fury that you did this

but also sisterly compassion
around your desperation
not to lose another mother in your partner.

having to give up two, not one
is surely enough to shatter anybody?

No wonder you didn't tell me
and now I know why you couldn't be
with your son

because you were guilty.
I didn't know you'd been waiting on death row
for he should have been two
not one.

Ride On II

I have found my way
to the other side of the world

everything I have clung to
has been turned on its head

like a flipped egg-timer
sand flows back into my body
and slowly I fill with a grounded security
completely unfamiliar to me.

It is thirty-one years to the day
since our birth-mother walked out on us.

I have delivered
my brother's possessions to his son
who I can now love
as one of us
as mine.

My horse is called Flynn.
Why have I waited so long for him?
These things take time.
There's no denying.

I follow the Arrow River.
The trees are gold, ruby, amber.
It's Autumn here, but in England it is Spring
and today feels like the first day.

I am wearing black
drinking sunshine deep into my skin.

We walk, trot, canter, jump.
I feel so natural
leaning into Flynn's tangled mane.

I remember so many things
breaking a horse in
getting back on again and again

galloping bareback from the paddock
laughing with Nick in Summer rain.

I remember about riding
about living.

I hadn't forgotten
I'd only forgotten
to take hold of the reins.

So now I ride on
and if you want to
you can come too.

Illustrations by Lara Varga

RIDE ON...

BY THE SAME AUTHOR

Poetry

Blind Peeping PotA Press 1995.

French Connections (with Tony Lewis-Jones) Firewater Press 1996.

Essays

'*On the Road to Recovery: Writing as Therapy for people in Recovery from Addiction*' in Writing Cures. Brunner-Routledge. 2004.

'*Using Poetry with Young People: Survive and Shine!*' in Poetry, Therapy and Emotional Life. Radcliffe Medical Press. 2005.